5

YOU WILL NEED: Balloons, newspaper, PVA glue, safety scissors, toilet roll tubes, sticky tape, cardboard, sequins, glitter, tissue paper or decorative raffia, tinsel.

Paint the unicorn's head and body a pale colour with darker hooves. Paint on eyes and nose, then leave it to dry.

6

To finish, decorate your unicorn with glitter and sequins, then stick on a mane and tail made from shredded rafia, tissue paper or tinsel.

THIS WOULD MAKE A GREAT MONEYBOX! JUST ADD A SLIT IN THE TOP AND A FLAP IN THE BOTTOM, SO YOU CAN GET YOUR MONEY OUT!

5

GINGERBREAD HOUSE

1

Use a cardboard box to make the house or construct the shape from pieces of cardboard as shown, taped together.

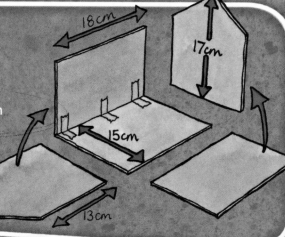

18cm

17cm

15cm

13cm

2

Make the roof by cutting two pieces of rectangular card to the width of the house. Tape one to the house as shown, then tape the other along the top like a hinge.

3

Cover the house in two layers of papier maché, leaving the roof flap uncovered so you can open it. Build up the edges with scrunched-up paper to look like icing and leave to dry.

6

Are you ready for an Art Attack?

WELCOME to a fantasty world, where you can meet a magical unicorn, make a gingerbread house and explore your very own fairytale castle! Follow the steps and let your imagination take over, as you create all kinds of weird and wonderful things, from gargoyle bookends to shimmering shapes you can stick on your window.

So let's have an Art Attack and visit the land of make-believe!

CONTENTS

Editor: Julie Scott
Designer: Darren Miles
Artists: Mary Hall and Paul Gamble
Model Maker: Angela Hart

MAGICAL UNICORN!

GIVE THIS FRIENDLY FELLOW A HOME AND HE MIGHT MAKE YOUR WISHES COME TRUE!

1 Blow up two balloons, one larger than the other. The bigger one is the body and the smaller one is the head. Cover both balloons in three layers of papier maché and leave them to dry.

2 Pop the balloons and remove them from the papier maché shells. Cut a strip of toilet roll tube about 4cm wide, then snip the side to make a curved strip. Tape this to the side of the body balloon to make the neck. Tape the head on its side to the neck.

3 Use four more toilet roll tubes to make the legs and tape them to the bottom of the body. Trim the tops of the toilet roll tubes at an angle to get a snug fit between the body and the legs.

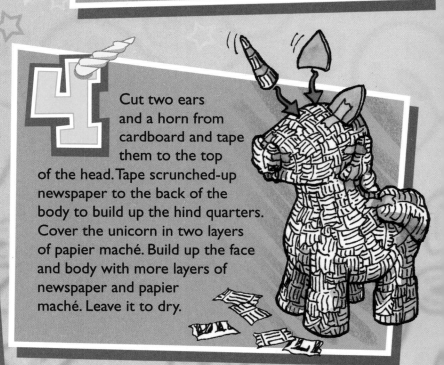

4 Cut two ears and a horn from cardboard and tape them to the top of the head. Tape scrunched-up newspaper to the back of the body to build up the hind quarters. Cover the unicorn in two layers of papier maché. Build up the face and body with more layers of newspaper and papier maché. Leave it to dry.

YOU WILL NEED: A cardboard box, safety scissors, cardboard, sticky tape, newspaper, PVA glue, paints, paintbrush, beads, pom-poms.

4 Paint the house an orangey-brown colour with white icing and leave it to dry.

5 Finally, decorate your gingerbread house with beads and pom-poms to look like sweets.

Fill the house with treats and give it to someone as a birthday present!

CAPTIVATING

PRINCE CHARMING

YOU WILL NEED:

Thin gold card, tape measure, safety scissors, sticky tape, pom-poms, fabric shapes, sparkly card, tinsel, PVA glue, cardboard box card, newspaper, paints, paintbrush.

CROWN

Ask an adult to measure round your head and help you cut a piece of gold card the right size. Cut points along one of the long sides and tape the two short sides together. Decorate with glitter glue, sequins, fabric shapes and pom-poms, and finish with a length of tinsel glued around the bottom edge.

SHIELD AND SWORD

Draw a shield and sword shape onto a piece of cardboard box card and cut them out. Cut extra strips of cardboard for the cross in the middle of the shield and the sword's handle and tape them into position. Cover with two layers of paper maché and leave them to dry. Paint as shown, then decorate with sequins.

Make up a crest of your own by painting pictures of things you're interested in, such as your favourite sport, or something to do with your home town.

COSTUMES!

PRETTY PRINCESS

YOU WILL NEED:
Thin gold card, tape measure, safety scissors, sticky tape, pom-poms, fabric shapes, sparkly card, tinsel, PVA glue, cardboard box card, newspaper, paints, paintbrush.

CROWN

Follow the instructions for making the Prince's crown, but instead of gluing tinsel around the bottom edge stick some glittery pipe cleaners to the top at the front as shown.

PENDANT

Cut a circle of gold card and decorate it with a fabric star, glitter glue and sequins. Wrap a glittery pipe cleaner around the edge, then stick a length of sparkly thread on so you can hang it round your neck.

RING

Cut a thin band of gold card big enough to wrap around one of your fingers and tape it closed. Cut a small heart from gold card and cover it with glue, then sprinkle it with glitter. When it's dry, decorate the heart with sequins.

TWINKLY TOWERS!

MAKE THIS MINATURE CASTLE AND WATCH
A MAGICAL DISPLAY OF SHOOTING STARS!

1 Ask an adult to help you find an empty jar with a lid. Make sure it's been washed out properly and soak it in warm, soapy water to remove any labels.

2 Use coloured modelling clay to make a miniature fairy castle in the inside of the lid. Make sure it's firmly attached to the lid so it doesn't fall out when you turn the jar upside down!

3 Ask an adult to fill the jar with a mixture of half water and half glycerine (from a chemist). Mix it thoroughly, then add some star-shaped sequins. Water on its own will work, too, but the stars will fall more quickly.

HOW ABOUT MAKING A DIFFERENT MODEL? YOU COULD MAKE SOME FLOWERS, A FAIRY OR EVEN A WIZARD!

4 Carefully lower the castle into the jar and screw the lid on firmly. Now turn it upside down and gently shake the jar – see how the stars swirl around the castle!

YOU WILL NEED:

A clean, empty jar with its lid, coloured modelling clay, small sequins or stars, glycerine.

TIP: store the jar the right way up (so the castle is upside-down) if you're not using it, to make sure it doesn't leak!

POT OF GOLD!

MAKE THIS MARVELLOUS MONEYBOX AND WATCH YOUR SAVINGS MULTIPLY LIKE MAGIC!

1 Blow up the balloon and cover it in three layers of papier maché. Leave it to dry, then burst the balloon and remove the pieces.

2 Trim down the top of the balloon to make a pot shape. Cut a rough shape for the base of the pot from thick cardboard, to look like the base of a sack. Tape the balloon to the base.

3 Draw a quarter of the way around a dinner plate onto thin card to make the curve of the rainbow and add a long, straight tail (this will be hidden inside the pot of gold). Cut it out, then use this as a template to make another piece exactly the same. Cut out another thin strip of card and tape all three pieces together as shown.

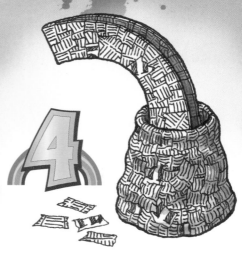

4 Tape the rainbow in place, then cover the whole thing with three layers of papier maché, building up around the base of the pot to make a sack shape. Leave it to dry.

5 Use a dry piece of sponge to dab on brown and yellow and white paint for the sack colour. Paint on a black cord with a brush and the word 'gold' in brown. Paint the rainbow and leave it to dry. Stick on large gold sequins or cut circles of card and paint them yellow. Glue them on when they are dry.

GOLD

PLACE A COIN AT THE TOP OF THE RAINBOW AND WATCH IT ROLL INTO THE POT AT THE BOTTOM!

GOLD

MOONLIGHT MOBILE!

WATCH THESE SPARKLY SPRITES DANCING IN THE MOONLIGHT!

1 Trace or photocopy the page opposite and stick it onto a piece of thin card.

YOU WILL NEED: Safety scissors, thin card, glue, felt–tip pens, glitter, string.

2 Colour in the pictures and add some glitter for extra sparkle! You could even stick on some sequins if you like.

3 Carefully cut out all the pieces and make a hole on each of the black dots. Ask an adult to help you with this.

4 Thread pieces of string through the holes to join the fairies and stars together, then tie these to the moon. Finally, thread another piece of string through the hole at the top of the moon and make a loop to hang it up.

FAIRYTALE CASTLE

KEEP YOUR DESK TIDY WITH THIS COOL CASTLE!

1 To make the base board, cut a shape with rounded edges from thick card. Cut pieces out of the end of a toilet roll tube to look like turrets, then arrange the other toilet roll and the two kitchen roll tubes as shown. Tape them together, then tape them to the base board. Cut a strip of toilet roll tube and tape it to the front to make the moat, as shown.

2  Cover the whole thing in two layers of papier maché., building up the edges of the two toilet roll tubes with extra layers. Leave it to dry.

3 Cut five circles of thin card to make the roofs. Snip into the centre of each circle and twist it into a pointed cone. Three of the roofs should fit over the top of the crisp tube and the kitchen roll tubes, the other two should slot inside the toilet roll tubes. Tape them in place, then cover them in two layers of papier maché.

4 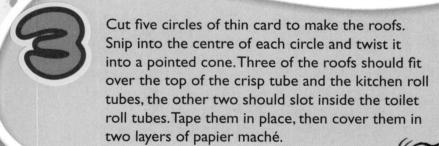 To make the bridge, cut a strip of thin card and tape it in place over the moat.

5

Paint your castle as shown, or choose your favourite, fairytale colours!

LEAVE THE ROOFS LOOSE INSTEAD OF TAPING THEM DOWN, SO YOU CAN POP IN YOUR PENS AND PENCILS!

OVER THE RAINBOW!

WHO WILL YOU SEND ON A SPARKLING JOURNEY?

1 Paint a picture like the one shown here. Paint the background pale blue to look like the sky, then add some fluffy white clouds and a yellow sun.

2 Next paint a big, colourful rainbow. Copy the one here to make sure the colours are in the right order!

3 When the paint is dry, squeeze PVA glue in a spiral pattern onto the sun and wiggly lines along the top of the clouds, then sprinkle on some gold and silver glitter.

4 Cut some drop shapes from tin foil and glue these to the picture to look like rain.

5 Ask an adult to help you cut along the top edge of the rainbow, not quite all the way to the edge of the picture (the rainbow should still be attached).

6 Choose which character you'd like in your picture and trace or photocopy the template. Stick it to a piece of thin card, colour it in and cut it out. Decorate it with glitter, if you like!

7 Cut a strip of thin card and stick your character to the top. Now slot the strip behind the rainbow and fix the end in place with a paper fastener.

YOU WILL NEED:

Paper, paints, paintbrush, glitter, scraps of tin foil, glue, thin card, safety scissors, paper fastener.

BEASTLY BOOKENDS

THIS PROUD PAIR OF GARGOYLES WILL KEEP YOUR BOOKS IN PERFECT ORDER!

1 Cut about 4cm off the height of the crisp tube and then fill it half full with clean pebbles. Tape over the opening, then scrunch up a ball of newspaper and tape over the end.

2 Loosely fold a sheet of dry newspaper and cut it up to make the arms and legs. Tape them to the tube as shown.

3 Cut out two wings from card and tape them to the side of the tube, then cut two round feet shapes and two ears and tape these in place, too.

4 Cover the whole thing with two layers of papier maché, building up the nose and mouth areas with extra layers. Build up the hands and feet in the same way, then leave it to dry.

THE OTHER GARGOYLE CAN LOOK SLIGHTLY DIFFERENT, WITH BIG EARS, POP-OUT EYES AND FANGS!

5 Use a dry piece of sponge to dab on grey, black and white paint. Make shadow areas in the armpits and leg creases by dabbing on black paint. Add highlights on the top lip and nose by dabbing on white paint.

YOU WILL NEED:

Two crisp tubes, pebbles, sticky tape, cardboard, newspaper, PVA glue, paints, paintbrush.

FABULOUS FRAMES!

GIVE YOUR FRIENDS THE ROYAL TREATMENT WITH THESE PRINCE AND PRINCESS PICTURE FRAMES!

 **1** Trace or photocopy the pictures opposite and stick them onto thin card.

YOU WILL NEED: Safety scissors, thin card, glue, felt-tip pens, sequins.

2 Colour in the pictures using felt-tip pens and stick on some sequins for extra sparkle!

 **3** Carefully cut around the edge of the pictures and cut out the spaces in the heads. You might need to ask an adult to help with this.

 **4** Now simply fix a photo to the back of the frame with sticky tape, making sure the face fits in the hole you've cut out.

MARVELLOUS MASK!

DISGUISE YOURSELF WITH THIS DECORATIVE MASK – IT'S PERFECT FOR A FANCY DRESS PARTY!

 1 Trace or photocopy the template below and stick it onto thin card.

 **2** Cut a strip of card and stick it to one side to use as a handle. You could use a lolly stick, a wooden kebab stick or a long straw instead.

 3 Paint or colour in your mask with felt-tip pens. Make it as colourful as you like! Gold or silver paint will give it a shimmery look.

 4 When it's dry, decorate it with glitter and sequins or anything else you like. Finally, tape some feathers to the back of the mask so they stick up above it.

Make it as fancy as you like!

How about old sweet wrappers, shiny buttons or pom-poms?

Collect different things to decorate your mask.

SHIMMERING SHAPES!

ADD SOME SPARKLE TO YOUR LIFE WITH THESE SUPER SHINY GLITTER STICKERS!

YOU WILL NEED: Paintbrush, PVA glue, glitter, a plastic surface.

1 Find a plastic surface, like an old tray. Check with an adult before you start.

2 Using an old paintbrush and PVA glue, make lots of different shapes. Paint the glue on quite thickly.

3 Sprinkle lots of glitter over the shapes and leave them to dry.

4 Carefully peel the shapes off the surface, then use them to decorate your window or a mirror!

If you fancy a change, simply peel off the stickers and stick them somewhere else!